Alicia Keys

Other books in the People in the News series:

Maya Angelou	Ashton Kutcher
Tyra Banks	Spike Lee
Glenn Beck	George Lopez
David Beckham	Tobey Maguire
Beyoncé	Eli Manning
Sandra Bullock	John McCain
Fidel Castro	Barack Obama
Kelly Clarkson	Michelle Obama
Hillary Clinton	Apolo Anton Ohno
Miley Cyrus	Danica Patrick
Ellen Degeneres	Nancy Pelosi
Johnny Depp	Katy Perry
Leonardo DiCaprio	Tyler Perry
Hilary Duff	Queen Latifah
Zac Efron	Daniel Radcliffe
Brett Favre	Condoleezza Rice
50 Cent	Rihanna
Jeff Gordon	Alex Rodriguez
Al Gore	Derrick Rose
Tony Hawk	J.K. Rowling
Salma Hayek	Shakira
Jennifer Hudson	Tupac Shakur
LeBron James	Will Smith
Jay-Z	Gwen Stefani
Derek Jeter	Ben Stiller
Steve Jobs	Hilary Swank
Dwayne Johnson	Justin Timberlake
Angelina Jolie	Usher
Jonas Brothers	Denzel Washington
Kim Jong II	Serena Williams
Coretta Scott King	Oprah Winfrey

Alicia
Keys

by Leanne K. Currie-McGhee

LUCENT BOOKS
A part of Gale, Cengage Learning

GALE
CENGAGE Learning·

Detroit • New York • San Francisco • New Haven, Conn • Waterville, Maine • London

GALE
CENGAGE Learning·

LIBRARY OF CONGRESS CATALOGING-IN-PUBLICATION DATA

Currie-McGhee, L. K. (Leanne K.)
  Alicia Keys / by Leanne K. Currie-McGhee.
    p. cm. -- (People in the news)
  Includes bibliographical references and index.
  ISBN 978-1-4205-0782-9 (hardcover)
1. Keys, Alicia--Juvenile literature. 2. Rhythm and blues musicians--United States--
Biography--Juvenile literature. I. Title.
  ML3930.K39C87 2012
  782.42164092--dc23
  [B]
                                                                    2012003264

Lucent Books
27500 Drake Rd
Farmington Hills MI 48331

ISBN-13: 978-1-4205-0782-9
ISBN-10: 1-4205-0782-6

Printed in the United States of America
1 2 3 4 5 6 7 16 15 14 13 12

Contents

Fame and celebrity are alluring. People are drawn to those who walk in fame's spotlight, whether they are known for great accomplishments or for notorious deeds. The lives of the famous pique public interest and attract attention, perhaps because their experiences seem in some ways so different from, yet in other ways so similar to, our own.

Newspapers, magazines, and television regularly capitalize on this fascination with celebrity by running profiles of famous people. For example, television programs such as *Entertainment Tonight* devote all their programming to stories about entertainment and entertainers. Magazines such as *People* fill their pages with stories of the private lives of famous people. Even newspapers, newsmagazines, and television news frequently delve into the lives of well-known personalities. Despite the number of articles and programs, few provide more than a superficial glimpse at their subjects.

Lucent's People in the News series offers young readers a deeper look into the lives of today's newsmakers, the influences that have shaped them, and the impact they have had in their fields of endeavor and on other people's lives. The subjects of the series hail from many disciplines and walks of life. They include authors, musicians, athletes, political leaders, entertainers, entrepreneurs, and others who have made a mark on modern life and who, in many cases, will continue to do so for years to come.

These biographies are more than factual chronicles. Each book emphasizes the contributions, accomplishments, or deeds that have brought fame or notoriety to the individual and shows how that person has influenced modern life. Authors portray their subjects in a realistic, unsentimental light. For example, Bill Gates—cofounder of the software giant Microsoft—has been instrumental in making personal computers the most vital tool of the modern age. Few dispute his business savvy, his perseverance, or his technical expertise, yet critics say he is ruthless in his dealings with competitors and driven more by his desire to maintain Microsoft's dominance in the computer industry than by an interest in furthering technology.

In these books, young readers will encounter inspiring stories about real people who achieved success despite enormous obstacles. Oprah Winfrey—one of the most powerful, most watched, and wealthiest women in television history—spent the first six years of her life in the care of her grandparents while her unwed mother sought work and a better life elsewhere. Her adolescence was colored by pregnancy at age fourteen, rape, and sexual abuse.

Each author documents and supports his or her work with an array of primary and secondary source quotations taken from diaries, letters, speeches, and interviews. All quotes are footnoted to show readers exactly how and where biographers derive their information and provide guidance for further research. The quotations enliven the text by giving readers eyewitness views of the life and accomplishments of each person covered in the People in the News series.

In addition, each book in the series includes photographs, annotated bibliographies, timelines, and comprehensive indexes. For both the casual reader and the student researcher, the People in the News series offers insight into the lives of today's newsmakers—people who shape the way we live, work, and play in the modern age.

A Veteran at Age Thirty

In 2011 Alicia Keys, just thirty years old, celebrated the anniversary of her first successful work as a musician. Ten years before, her first album, *Songs in A Minor*, debuted to critical and commercial success. It made her millions of dollars and propelled her to superstardom.

Songs in A Minor was released in June 2001 after Keys had worked on it for several years. The album, a mixture of jazz, R&B, and soul, premiered at number one on the charts and ended up winning five Grammy Awards along with millions of fans.

Commemorating a Hit Album

Because it changed her life and launched her career, Keys wanted to commemorate the tenth anniversary of *Songs in A Minor*. To celebrate, Keys and her record label decided to release special anniversary collector's edition of *Songs in A Minor*. Released in June 2011, the edition contains not only the original album's songs but also unreleased songs, a video of Keys playing a concert, and a documentary created for the edition that includes new interviews with Keys. On her website, Keys shared the news about the anniversary edition of the album with her fans. "I can't believe it's been ten years since this record," Keys wrote. "I am so blessed to have fans like all of you, who've embraced my songs with such heart. THANK YOU for all these amazing years!!"[1]

Keys performs in Paris as part of her "Piano & I: A One Night Only Event" tour to mark the 10th anniversary of her album Songs in A Minor.

As part of the anniversary celebration, Keys also went on a limited tour. "I can't think of a better way to celebrate the 10th anniversary of 'Songs in A Minor', than by holding a special, intimate concert for my fans. It's my absolute favorite way to perform," she said. "There is something so special about just me on my piano connecting with the audience. It brings me back to the very beginning when I could only perform with a keyboard and to now be able to take it back to the essence of who I am with this show, it is so exciting."[2]

The tour, titled Piano & I: A One Night Only Event, included concerts in Paris, London, New York City, and Los Angeles. The performances featured just Keys and her piano, with no backup vocals or instruments, playing the entire *Songs in A Minor* album, along with other hits from later albums. She also performed a few new songs that had not yet been released on any album.

The performances garnered some of Keys's best live-tour reviews. According to the *New York Daily News*, she did what she does best: She simply played the piano and sang. Instead of having glitzy sets or big theatrical numbers like most other concerts of the day, Keys's vocals and piano playing were the focus of the tour.

A Decade of Work

Songs in A Minor launched Keys's career and enabled her to not only make more music but to also branch into other areas of the entertainment industry. Keys acted in movies, codirected a film for television, coproduced a Broadway play, and wrote a book. She also helped create a charity for Africans affected by AIDS (acquired immunodeficiency syndrome).

Most of Keys's ventures have resulted in success. Many say that success is due to both her talents and her work ethic. After *Songs in A Minor*, Keys released four more commercially successful albums, won several Grammy Awards, and raised millions of dollars for her charity. On the personal front, she married and had a child.

Keys does not show any signs of slowing down. She continues to develop professionally and create new plans and ideas for the future. What happens next is up to her.

Chapter 1

What Music Means

Alicia Keys was born Alicia Augello Cook on January 25, 1981. Her parents were Teresa Augello, a paralegal and actress, and Craig Cook, a flight attendant. Shortly after Keys was born, Cook left the family. "I'd been dating Alicia's father for a while, and when I told him I wanted to keep the baby he said he had other plans—and they weren't with us," recalled Augello. "So I knew I'd have to go it alone."[3]

This left Augello on her own to raise and provide for her daughter. According to Keys, her mother did not complain, and she made sure her daughter had the opportunity to prosper. Keys's mother taught her to depend on herself and deal with life. "She's been a huge influence on me. I saw a woman handling herself in a bad situation. If she'd been cowering under pressure, depending on a man to take care of her, I know I'd have grown up to be a whole other person,"[4] said Keys.

Keys's mother also instilled in her the value of hard work. Early on, Keys saw, from her mother's efforts, that hard work is the key to accomplish anything. Her mother worked two, sometimes three jobs, in order to support them. "She worked around the clock. I don't know how she stood up from day to day," said Keys. "If there was a big trial [that Augello worked on as a paralegal], she'd come home at 3 A.M., then get up at 6 A.M. and keep going."[5]

Due to her parents' ethnicity, Keys is Italian, Scottish, Irish, and African American, but she mostly identifies with being African American. "My background made me a broad person, able to relate to different cultures," Keys said. "But any woman of color, even a mixed color, is seen as black in America. So that's how I regard myself."[6]

Keys is accompanied by her mother, Teresa Augello, at a movie premiere in 2007. Augello raised Alicia as a single mother.

Hell's Kitchen

Keys grew up in Hell's Kitchen, a neighborhood in the Manhattan area of New York City. It is unknown how the area got its name, but it has been referred to as Hell's Kitchen since the late 1800s. At the turn of the twentieth century gangs began to live in Hell's Kitchen, and it became a violent place. Because of the gangs and their fights, the area became one of New York's toughest areas. During Keys's childhood, it was still a rough place to live, but she learned how to take care of herself. "You'd often find yourself in situations where you wished you had something more than just your hands. So I would carry around a little shank, a homemade knife. When my mother found it she was so upset and couldn't understand why I had it," Keys said. "I needed a knife, just in case. I definitely understand that feeling of wanting to protect yourself."[7]

Keys and her mother lived in Hell's Kitchen because they did not have much money. Her mother worked several part-time jobs in addition to auditioning for acting and musical roles in order to provide for the two of them. They lived simply in a modest one-bedroom apartment. Even with their limited finances, Augello saved enough money to pay for acting and dance classes for Keys.

Opening Worlds

Augello thought that Keys was talented in many areas and wanted her to develop these talents. Augello herself was talented in acting, dancing, and music and attempted to build a career in the theater. After graduating from New York University, she was cast in a theater production, but then she got pregnant with Keys. At this point she continued working in the theater part-time but decided to get more stable jobs to make a steady income.

Augello wanted her daughter to attend classes so she could develop her talents, but she also wanted Keys involved in artistic endeavors to keep her busy and out of trouble. She enrolled Keys in drama, acting, and gymnastics classes. Keys liked these classes and performed as early as four years old when she sang in her kindergarten's version of the musical *The Wiz*. When she was five, her mother enrolled her in piano and ballet classes. "Being a single parent raising her in the city, I tried to give her every opportunity, just so she could find out what her muse was,"[8] Augello said. When Keys was just five years old, Augello managed to get her a role on the television comedy *The Cosby Show*.

Keys was drawn most to music. According to Augello, Keys's grandmother is part of the reason Keys became interested in the piano. "My own mother would come and stay if I had to work out of town. She was a pianist and a singer and encouraged Alicia's interest in music," Augello said. "When she was seven, Alicia started taking classical piano lessons. She studied under the Suzuki method, where the parent must be involved, so I'd go to practice with her."[9]

Her mother could not afford to buy a piano, but Keys remembers that they got lucky when a friend decided to get rid of hers. Keys

Augello was an aspiring actress and dancer who chose a more stable career when Keys was born. She encouraged her daughter's interest in the arts from an early age.

and her mother immediately offered to take it. "A friend was getting rid of this old, brown upright piano she rarely played, and she agreed to let us have it if we'd move it from her apartment," Keys recalled. "We used the piano as a divider between our living room and my bedroom. That gift is one of the main reasons I'm playing today."[10]

Finding Her Music

Keys, who admits that she does not often express her feelings verbally, learned to express herself through music. At age seven, she wrote her first song using the piano. She credits God with helping her find her way through music. "God was with us. I wrote my first song—a tune about my grandfather, my Fa-Fa, who'd passed away—on that piano," Keys remembered. "I'd just returned from seeing [the film] *Philadelphia*, and it was after the movie that, for the first time, I could express how I felt through the music."[11]

Keys's piano teacher taught her using the Suzuki method, which is a rigid Japanese method that includes parental involvement, loving encouragement, and constant repetition. Her teacher mainly focused on classical music. "Classical piano totally helped me to be a better songwriter and a better musician," Keys said. "You know, I understood music. I knew the fundamentals of music. And I understood how to put things together and pull it together and change it. The dedication that it took to study classical music is a big reason why I have anything in this life I think."[12]

Keys also learned about music by listening to it, and she developed an appreciation for all different types of music. She learned about classical music during her lessons. Keys liked the composer Chopin's music the best because his pieces are slow and romantic. For jazz and rhythm and blues she was drawn to artists Curtis Mayfield, Sly and the Family Stone, Aretha Franklin, Nina Simone, Billie Holiday, and Ella Fitzgerald, all of whom would influence her musical style.

Keys performs on the piano, which she began playing when she was five years old. She wrote her first song at age seven.

Performing Arts School

When Keys was twelve years old, she entered the Professional Performing Arts School of Manhattan, which focused on performing arts, such as music, acting, and dance, while also providing a traditional education. At this school, Miss Aziza, a pianist and composer, introduced Keys to songwriting and producing. Keys discovered she loved making her own music and fully concentrated on that. She was serious about her musical development while at school. Chris Glover, who later became the musician Penguin Prison, attended the school with Keys. "I was in [the] gospel choir with her," he stated. "She was more mature than other kids. The teacher of our gospel choir treated her differently [than] everyone else because she was more grown up."[13]

While at school, Keys was influenced by even more types of music by artists such as Duke Ellington, Beethoven, Miles Davis, Stevie Wonder, Carole King, and Scott Joplin. At thirteen years old she discovered soul music with singer Marvin Gaye's album *What's Going On*, and it later influenced the type of music she produced. "It just hit me like a rock over the head," Keys said. "I had never heard a body of music like that, so in tune with people and reality and consciousness, socially and politically and in love with stillness and then turmoil. It was like everything that you ever have felt at one point or another all in one, bam!"[14]

Teenage Rebellion

While at school Keys's independence developed. At times this was difficult for her mother, who said "I'd be voicing my discontent with 'You shouldn't do that,' and she'd [Alicia] be voicing her claims with things like 'Age is just a number.'"[15] Keys's mother worried about her constantly.

One reason that the two clashed, according to Keys, was that they dealt with emotions differently. While her mother was direct and open about how she felt and what bothered her, Alicia kept her feelings to herself. She would internalize her anger until something provoked her, and then it came out in ways that hurt her mother, such as running off without telling her mother where she was going.

Keys and Augello attend the Grammy Awards in 2002. Keys admits to clashing with her mother frequently when she was a teenager, which strained their relationship for a time.

Remembering that time period, Keys now realizes how much she emotionally hurt her mother. "I can only think I must've tortured my mother. I wouldn't call her or come home when I said I would. And when I did, I'd prance in like I owned the place. I was terrible," Keys said. "Of course, we'd then argue for ages, and I'd leave again."[16] The relationship between Keys and her mother was strained for awhile. Later, after Keys moved out, they were both able to forgive one another and move forward.

Braids As Self-Expression

Alicia Keys's sense of style, like her music, is unique. When she became famous, she did not change her appearance. She had been wearing her hair in braids since the age of fifteen, and she kept the style even after becoming famous. "Somebody braided my hair for me and I loved it," she recalled. "It was just so easy for me because my hair is, like it's crazy. It has a mind of its own. It doesn't lie down and if I try to wear it straight, it doesn't stay because it's frizzy. I like my hair braided because it can be any design and style that I want. And it's pretty and it's different."

Quoted in Lynn Norment. "Alicia Keys Sounds off on Men, Love & Fame." *Ebony*, January 2004.

Keys said that one bonus of that time was that it resulted in her writing and playing her own songs. She would take the feelings she had after fighting with her mother and let them out in her songs. Using music to express her feelings became a practice that Keys would continue throughout her life.

Getting Discovered

Outside of school Keys continued to develop her music by writing. At age fourteen she began singing in a three-girl group called EmBishion in a Police Athletic League center in Harlem, New York. She also worked with a vocal coach. Her coach, Conrad Robinson, saw Keys's musical potential, and one day Robinson invited his brother, Jeff Robinson, who was a rhythm-and-blues manager, to listen to Keys. "My brother had asked me to come by and hear this young girl," Jeff recalled. "He said she was pretty but very talented. I stopped by the studio one day and heard her sing and play the piano, and I was totally blown away."[17] Jeff encouraged Keys to pursue a career as a solo artist. Keys realized that Jeff shared her vision for her music, and he became her manager.

A Record Deal

Jeff Robinson put together showcases for Keys so that the heads of various recording labels could hear her play. A bidding war, which is when different labels compete for an artist with offers, occurred because each one wanted her. Keys had difficulty deciding which offer was best. Ultimately, a piano swayed her decision.

One of the recording labels that Keys met with was Columbia Records. Keys recalled,

Alicia Keys attends a record release party in 2003 with Kerry Brothers, who was her collaborator when she first signed with Columbia in the mid-1990s.

Columbia brought me in to play in this gorgeous building that looks out over Manhattan. I was on, like, the 579th floor with this white piano.... The whole room was white and glass, and I'd never seen anything like it. I was like "Wow." So I played my little songs and everyone was excited. I was in heaven. Then the exec cleared everybody out and said to me, "If you sign with us, I'll give you this piano." All I had at home was my broken-down room divider. He might as well have been offering me diamonds. The guy says, "I'll give you 15 minutes," then he walks out. It was a game. It was a $26,000 piano—and I signed with Columbia.[18]

Keys began working on her first album but she soon encountered difficulties. She had trouble developing songs. After a few months, Columbia was asking to hear her songs, but she was not ready. Keys felt pressure to fulfill her contract but was not sure what to do. Her collaborator (who can help write, arrange, and/or produce songs), Kerry Brothers, made a suggestion. He told her that she needed her own equipment to produce, arrange, and record her songs. Keys decided he was right and bought her own equipment, such as audio mixers, microphones, and recording software.

At the same time, Keys moved out of her mother's apartment and into a sixth-floor apartment in Harlem. Initially she made her bedroom into a recording studio, but the neighbors complained about the noise. She briefly moved to a place in New Jersey that did not work out and then found a house in Queens. She converted the basement into KrucialKeys Studios. With her own equipment and her own place, she created her own album and was happy with the type of music she developed. Unfortunately for her, Columbia was not excited by her results.

Leaving Colombia

When Keys played her music for Columbia executives, they were not satisfied with her music or her look. Keys said, "My manager was ecstatic, but some people at the label [Columbia] were saying, 'What's this? It's kind of soulful. Where are the pop smashes?'

They wanted my hair blown out and flowing, my dresses shorter. And they wanted me to lose weight."[19]

Keys did not want to change her looks or her music. She was not interested in creating pop music and wanted to continue making her own music, which was more blues and soul. "Once I saw that these people were completely disrespecting my musical creativity," said Keys. "I was devastated and crushed, like a blooming flower that's trampled on. Nothing hurts more. I'm fortunate that my manager was confident."[20]

Getting out of a music contract is not easy but Keys's manager was able to get Keys out of hers. He even managed to get ownership of the music she created while she was under the contract. By late 1998, Keys was no longer with Columbia.

New Beginnings

As he was working to get Keys out of her contract, Robinson was also working to get her a new record label, one that appreciated her style of music. Eventually he managed to set up a meeting

Jeff Robinson, Augello, and Keys pose with Clive Davis, right, founder of J Records who signed Keys to the label after she left Columbia.

with Clive Davis, founder of New York–based J Records, an imprint of Bertelsmann Music Group. Robinson told Davis that Keys was a singer-songwriter of rare talent. He explained that she had a deal with Columbia Records, and it was not working out because Columbia wanted to change her material. Davis agreed to meet with Keys.

After meeting with Keys and listening to her play her own compositions, Davis immediately sensed she was a special artist. As soon as she was released from Columbia, Davis signed Keys to his record label. Keys agreed because she felt that Davis understood her, and he promised her creative control. "My first meeting with Clive was great," Keys recalled. "I'd never had anyone of his stature ask me how I saw myself, and what I wanted to do."[21] Keys began to record her music for J Records.

While she was recording her album, Keys also continued with her studies. She graduated as valedictorian from high school at age sixteen and was accepted to Columbia University. In all areas of her life, her hard work was paying off. Now she just needed to focus on the direction she wanted to go.

Chapter 2

A Successful Beginning

Alicia Keys figured out what she wanted to do in her life before she was twenty years old. Her goal was to become a successful musician, who produced soulful, meaningful music. Keys decided to get rid of any distractions from her music. She decided that college was one of the distractions.

Keys had started attending Columbia University while working on her first album. Shortly after she began school, Keys realized that she could not fully devote herself to her music and to college. Her music career included late-night studio sessions, which made it difficult to get up in the morning to go to class and she was tired when she tried to study. "I was always good in school, I knew how to do just enough to do what I had to do . . . but Columbia is a whole 'nother ball game!" Keys explained. "I was coming in from the studio at four in the morning and getting up at eight to try and do my homework on the train into my classes—no way! I was the worst student ever at that point in my life, and I was so stressed."[22] She decided to leave college and focus on her career.

Devotion to the Album

After leaving school, Keys spent the majority of her time working on her first album. She took a long time working on the album because she wanted to make sure that the music and lyrics were

Keys poses with her piano after the release of her first album, Songs in A Minor, *in 2001.*

just the way she envisioned. The time she took to work on the album helped her develop as an artist. "[It] allowed me to become a better songwriter," said Keys. "It allowed me to become a better musician because I wasn't stifled. Now, when I go into a studio with someone like Jermaine Dupri [who produced the album song "Girlfriend"], I'm confident [enough] in myself and my sound that now we can both bring something to the table."[23]

In Keys's first album, many of her feelings are expressed in her lyrics. She wrote "Troubles," which is a song that many consider one of the album's most affecting songs. The verses in "Troubles" talk about feeling scared and sad but the chorus is more uplifting, providing hope. Keys explained that when she wrote the song,

> I had already moved out of my mother's house, and I still would come back periodically, especially when I would feel lost or unbalanced or alone. She would probably be working and I would sit at the piano. Everything that I said in the verses was exactly how I felt, and what was said in

Keys rehearses in Beverly Hills, California, before one of many appearances to promote **Songs in A Minor,** *which was a commercial and critical success.*

the chorus was what I felt like God would be saying to me. I almost wanted to call it "Conversations With God."[24]

Keys explained that the piano ballad "Fallin'" represents her thoughts about relationships and how they affect people. "[It] is about the ins and outs of a relationship. Sometimes, you're completely head-over-heels in love with someone, and sometimes you can't stand that person. You fall in and out, sometimes it goes back and forth, and that's just what relationships are about,"[25] Keys explained. "Fallin'" would become one of the album's most popular songs.

Other songs on her album are personal because they are from her childhood. She wrote both "Butterflyz" and "The Life" before she was fourteen. She revised and updated these songs for the album.

The album, titled *Songs in A Minor*, is a mix of Keys's favorite types of music—jazz, blues, pop, and classical. She created different songs on the album using these types of music. For example, the first song on the album, "Piano & I," begins with a combination of composer Beethoven's "Moonlight Sonata" and a hip-hop beat. "The album is a fusion of my classical training, meshed with what I grew up listening to," Keys explained. "My music is a fusion of the things I've been exposed to and drawn from and my life experiences."[26]

Songs in A Minor Debuts

Before the album's release, J Records founder Clive Davis booked Keys for several interviews and musical performances to generate interest in her upcoming album. First, he booked Keys on *The Tonight Show with Jay Leno*, where she performed live. Davis then wrote a letter to talk-show host Oprah Winfrey and asked if Keys could perform on her show, *The Oprah Winfrey Show*, along with musicians Jill Scott and India Arie. Key's performance on the show caused preorders for her album to double that night.

J Records released *Songs in A Minor* on June 5, 2001. The album was an immediate success. It debuted at number one on the Billboard 200 chart and sold over 236,000 copies in its first week. Eventually it would sell over 6.2 million copies in the United States and 12 million copies worldwide.

"Fallin'" was the first single released from the album, and it also succeeded commercially. The song peaked at number one on the Billboard Hot 100 and Hot R&B/Hip-Hop Songs charts. "Fallin'" remained atop these charts for six and four weeks, respectively. It became the most-played song in the United States at the time, and the Recording Industry Association of America certified it gold, meaning the song had sold five hundred thousand copies. *Songs in A Minor* also received mainly positive responses from critics.

Songs in A Minor Misnamed?

Despite its title, *Songs in A Minor* has only one song, "Jane Doe," in the key of A minor. Also, *Songs in A Minor* was not the planned title of the album. Originally it was titled *Soul Stories in A Minor*, but record executives were concerned the title would limit its exposure to radio stations that only played soul music.

Rolling Stone magazine named *Songs in A Minor* the second-best album of 2001, while ranking it number 95 on its list of the best albums of the decade. Steve Jones, a music reviewer for the newspaper *USA Today*, wrote,

> Rarely has a newcomer lived up to the hype the way Keys does. From the almost operatic piano intro to the minimalistic outro, the 19-year-old singer never ceases to surprise and delight. She taps into the blues, soul, jazz and even classical music to propel haunting melodies and hard-driving funk. The stunning first single, Fallin', a bluesy ode to self-destructive love, is only a teaser for what she has to offer. Keys already has a musical, artistic and thematic maturity that many more experienced artists never achieve. That she's only just begun makes it even more amazing.[27]

Other critics, such as John Mulvey of the Yahoo! Music website, praised the album for using classic soul melodies along with more modern techniques. *Songs in A Minor* also earned a score of 78 on Metacritic, a website that uses reviews by critics to rate entertainment, such as movies, television shows, electronic games, and music, with a score between 0 to 100 based on reviews from mainstream critics.

Her First Tour

To promote her album, Keys went on tour, playing her songs in front of live audiences. From January to August 2002 she performed more than fifty concerts across the United States. In preparing for her tour, Keys considered her audience as she decided how and what to play at her concerts:

Keys performs in Las Vegas, Nevada, in 2002 as part of her concert tour to promote **Songs in A Minor.**

I think about who is going to be in my audience and how is it going to affect them. I'm 20, so I'm on a certain level. But at the same time there are people who are in my audience who are 11, 12. They're looking at me as what is cool or what they should be like. It's something that I have to be conscious of, and I don't mind being conscious of it. But first and foremost I have to come from the place within, and make sure that I love it and that it means something to me.[28]

Keys also spent a lot of time preparing for each performance. Toward the beginning of her tour, she played at Radio City Music Hall in New York City. Jon Pareles, a reporter for the *New York Times* newspaper, interviewed Keys a few days before her concert and discovered how intense her practices were. The day he met with Keys, she began rehearsing at 3 P.M., and around 11:30 P.M. she called for a complete run-through of the set (playing the concert from beginning to end), minus a solo piano interlude she would add onstage. By 1:00 A.M., she finished playing. The musicians she played with headed home while she remained, discussing any suggestions and changes with Jeff Robinson, her manager, and Peter Edge, executive vice president at J Records. Around 2:00 A.M., Pareles went home but Keys remained, working on the concert's choreography.

Her First Recordings

Alicia Key's first recording was the song, "The Little Drummer Girl". It is one of the songs on the 1996 Christmas album *The 12 Soulful Nights of Christmas* for the record label So So Def. She also cowrote and recorded a song titled "Dah Dee Dah (Sexy Thing)," which is on the soundtrack of the 1997 film, *Men in Black*.

Keys's hard work paid off. She played to sold-out audiences and received positive reviews, such as one in the *Guardian* newspaper in London, which read, "Despite the obvious appeal of the album, Keys truly comes into her own when she plays live. A sell-out show at London's intimate Scala last week confirmed the arrival of an artist of effortless charm and preternatural cool. Still only 20, she won over an intrigued audience with a display of easy grace and spectacular charisma."[29]

During her performances, Keys played songs from her album, but she made some musical changes and additions to them. She interspersed her songs with other music, such as classic compositions. "Onstage, she invariably starts with a little Beethoven," wrote Pareles of her concert in New York. "From there, she moves into rhythm-and-blues that's accessorized with hip-hop scratching, jazz scat-singing and glimmers of gospel. Within her songs, she plays virtually every female role in pop's vocabulary. As a girlfriend, she can be loyal, jealous, lusty, spurned or about to say goodbye; as her own woman, she balances fear and uncertainty against tenacity."[30]

Accolades for *Songs in A Minor*

Keys's first album received many awards. In February 2002, she received five Grammy Awards. The National Academy of Recording Arts and Sciences presents the Grammy Awards annually in a televised ceremony to recognize outstanding achievement in the music industry. Keys's awards were for Song of the Year, Best Female R&B Vocal Performance, Best R&B Song for "Fallin'," Best New Artist, and Best R&B Album. She became the second female solo artist in the history of the awards to win five awards in the same year.

Also in 2002 Keys received the BET Award for Best New Artist of the Year. The BET Awards, established in 2001 by the Black Entertainment Television network, celebrate African Americans and other minorities in music, acting, sports, and other areas of performance.

Keys poses at the 2002 Grammy Awards with the five awards she won that year, including Song of the Year, Best Female R&B Vocal Performance, Best R&B Song, Best New Artist, and Best R&B Album.

Continuing Work

As her album became successful, Keys got involved in other endeavors, such as helping to create the music videos for her songs. She wanted the videos to be unique. The video for "Fallin'," directed by Chris Robinson, does not include any dancing, because Keys wanted to focus on the story told by the song. In the video Keys plays a woman visiting her boyfriend in jail; the idea came from a news story Keys read about the girlfriend of a drug dealer who was convicted by association and sent to prison. At the time, Keys said, "I'm writing to her now, because I'm feeling what she's going through. That could be me in there."[31]

Keys also found the time to work with other performers. In 2002 she worked with singer Christina Aguilera on Aguilera's album *Stripped*. They sang the song "Impossible" together. Keys also wrote and coproduced the song and provided the background vocals.

Aside from music, Keys took on some acting roles during this time. In 2001 she had a small cameo in the TV show *Charmed*. Following that she also played a small role on an episode of *American Dreams*.

Not a Diva

Becoming famous changes a person's life. Some famous people expect special treatment just because they are famous. Keys says she does not see herself as a diva that deserves special treatment from others. "I hate the word," Keys said in an interview. "All of a sudden every singer who is successful is a diva. I think it's so fake. I'm not a diva. I'm who I am in interviews. And who I am on TV is who I am. It's not a game. It's not a joke. It's not a marketing scheme. It's not something I go to classes to learn how to do. I'm probably the most low-maintenance, easygoing person ever. I like to have good energy and I like to call people my friends. And I like to keep it like that."[32]

Becoming famous can also cause people to become very self-conscious about how they look. Keys claims this is not true for her. Although she exercises, Keys does not try to stay extremely

Keys has publicly noted her comfort with the shape of her body; unlike other famous performers, she does not feel the need to be "super skinny."

skinny as many famous female performers feel they should. "I'm very happy with my body," she said. "And I'm happy that I'm not super skinny. Sometimes I've gotten photographs back and people have literally shaven off pieces of me, and I tell them to put it back. I'm not ashamed of what I am and that I have curves and that I'm thick, like my body."[33]

Keys's success also led to a great amount of money. Like fame, money can also change people and their priorities. Keys was conscious to not let the money change what was important to her. She said,

> Simplicity makes me happy. I really like to live my life in a low-key fashion. I see what happens when one gets very attached to material things. That's just not what my life is. That's not what I love and that's not what makes me feel good. What makes me feel good are the simple things in life, like somebody I can really talk to, when I'm not concerned about whether they are going to betray me. My life is rich because I have those kinds of people in my life.[34]

Being in the Spotlight

Fame did change Keys in one way: It made her aware of how others, particularly young people, view her. She considers herself a role model and says that she conducts herself accordingly. In 2002 she talked about how she does not like the blatant sexuality that is often in modern music, videos, television shows, and movies. "Everything is just thrown on your lap from the time that you're 3," she said. "The Internet and the TV and the videos and the movies and everything is just like a big soft-porn industry, the entire world. If your elders are acting like that's what they want to do, how are you supposed to think anything else?"[35] Instead of writing sexually exploitive songs, Keys keeps her songs true to what is important to her—feelings and emotions and thoughts about life.

Keys is direct about her beliefs and feelings, and sometimes her comments were unpopular with the public. In New York she was interviewed by *Rolling Stone* just a few days after the September 11, 2001, terrorist attacks on the United States. She and the interviewer discussed the crowds in the city that were waving flags in support of the country. Keys admitted that she did not feel the patriotism that the crowds did. "All day I been seein' everyone rockin' flags in they hats and on the street, and I'm torn," she said. "I look at that flag, and I'm not able to completely go there for some reason. I see lies in that flag. I can't suddenly be all patriotic. But this is about human life beyond any country or flag. That's why it makes me feel so strange. Because I'm so torn, and there's so many layers involved."[36] Keys expressed heartfelt sympathy for all those affected by the attacks and horror at its occurrence, but these feelings did not overcome her conflict about being patriotic. She explained that because of the past treatment of black people by the United States in slavery and the struggle for civil rights, it was hard for her to feel the level of patriotism others were showing.

Importance of Others

Once Keys became famous she decided to use her fame to help others. In 2003, following the success of her first album and tour, Keys went on a trip to Africa. While there, she saw the terrible impact that AIDS was having on the country's population. AIDS had left more than 12 million children orphaned and 25 million people dead from 1987 to 2012. She saw firsthand that AIDS was orphaning children, devastating communities, and stifling economic progress. Keys decided to do something to help.

Keys and Leigh Blake, a longtime AIDS activist and film/TV producer, cofounded Keep a Child Alive (KCA) in 2002, a nonprofit organization that works to provide life-saving antiretroviral drugs to children and their families affected by AIDS in Africa and India.

To raise funds for KCA, Keys has been the cohost and musical director for KCA's annual Black Ball every year since 2004. The fund-raiser takes place in both New York and London. Over the years, Keys brought together famous musicians, such as Bono of U2, Kanye West, Damian Marley, David Bowie, Lenny Kravitz,

Keys arrives at the 2005 Black Ball fundraiser event for Keep a Child Alive, a charity she co-founded to provide medicine and support to people in Africa and India who are affected by HIV/AIDS.

Angelique Kidjo, John Mayer, Paul Simon, Nas, Common, and John Legend to help raise money and AIDS awareness. The funds raised have helped build clinics, pay for hospital staff, and provide food and care for the orphaned children. "It's amazing to return to Africa and witness those who were so sickly they literally were near death, being brought back to life because of the medical care they were able to receive," Keys said. "Just knowing that your time and effort has helped build pediatric wings in hospitals and supply medicine to those who might not otherwise receive it, gives me a real sense of purpose."[37]

Keys combined her work for KCA with her musical career. After her trip to Africa, she felt inspired to create her second album and hoped that it would reflect her growth as a person and as a musician.

Chapter 3

Onward and Upward

After such a successful first album, Keys could have sat back and enjoyed her success. Instead, she focused on creating her second album. She wanted this album to reflect her new experiences in life and in music. She began to work on the album in 2002 and continued throughout 2003.

Making a Second Album

Creating a second album after a very successful first album can be a nerve racking process for musicians. They often feel pressure to live up to the expectations of fans and critics. According to those who worked with her, Keys did not seem nervous about her second album. She seemed more concerned about whether or not it would reflect everything she was feeling. "I think she was more anxious than anything, 'cause she has so much to say," said guitarist Dwayne Wiggins, who first worked with Keys in the late 1990s, while she was with Columbia Records. "She'd been held back for so long, she was just ready to go, like a Ferrari in the slow lane."[38]

When she started on the album, Keys had the beginnings for many songs, but she was open to ideas from others. She brought over fifty different musicians into her sessions to play and compose. Some of her collaborators were Kanye West, and Stokley Williams from the band Mint Condition. "Kanye is really

Kanye West, left, was one of many musicians Keys collaborated with on **The Diary of Alicia Keys,** *her second album.*

a soulful brother, so we connected immediately," Keys said. "For me, the music that I love the most is the music from the '60s and '70s. It's just innovative—it's fresh, it's sweet. It's real feelings and emotions. A lot of this album feels like that to me. I like to call it 'Back to the Future.'"[39]

Keys kept the atmosphere at the sessions relaxed in order to bring out everyone's creativity. She made sure her studio had both modern and vintage instruments, so the musicians could try different sounds until they got the one they wanted. "We jammed a lot in the studio," said Andre Harris, from the production duo Dre & Vidal, who collaborated on the album. "We had live drums, live bass guitars, quite a few live instruments. We started sampling each other. It was a relaxed atmosphere and it was all about the music."[40]

As relaxed as the sessions were, the musicians remember how serious Keys was about the music. She had definite ideas about what she wanted on the album. One of the ideas Keys brought to Easy Mo Bee, one of the musicians working on the album, was to remake "If I Were Your Woman," by the group Gladys Knight and the Pips. Keys wanted to put the song's lyrics to a different familiar melody. She liked what Easy had done with the melody of another song, Isaac Hayes's "Walk on By" and wanted to try the same melody. "I was concerned about combining two melodies, like what key is she gonna do it in, how's it gonna work?" Easy recalled. "We started working on it from scratch, and as I'm making the track, she's sitting there singing it. I'm seeing her sitting in the chair at the board, half-smiling, singing. That told me it would work."[41]

A True Diary

Keys called her second album *The Diary of Alicia Keys*, and it is a personal work in which Keys lets her private thoughts come out in the music. "It's really, truly a diary," stated Wiggins. "Not many people would put their diaries out there, and I'm shocked that she did. People can feel the passion and pain in the music. It's almost like a reality show on wax. It's one of the most genuine things out there."[42]

At the end of the recording sessions, Keys was happy, because she felt the music reflected who she was. "When the album was completed I was ecstatic because I really felt the energy of the songs and hearing them as one piece of work, I was finally able to say, 'Yes, this is who I am right now,'" Keys said. "I'm so proud, happy, and excited that I could offer this music to the world."[43]

An Immediate Success

J Records released *The Diary of Alicia Keys* in December 2003. Like *Songs in A Minor*, it was an immediate commercial success. The album sold 618,000 copies during the first week of release in the United States, and the Recording Industry Association of America certified it seven-times platinum. It debuted at number one on the Billboard 200 chart. It sold two times more albums in its first week than *Songs in A Minor*.

Just a Kid

In 2006 Alicia Keys appeared on the children's television show, *BackYardigans*. She provided the voice for the animated character Mommy Martian in the musical episode "Mission from Mars." "After speaking with kids who said they loved the BackYardigans, I knew this would be a great project for me to get involved in," said Keys. "Working alongside my niece was so much fun and the people at Nick Jr. [Nickelodeon Jr] helped to make it a great experience. I can't wait to see it all put together to make one great episode." Keys also appeared on *Sesame Street* and sang a version of "Fallin'" with Elmo in 2005.

Quoted in Stephanie. "Alicia Keys Guest Stars on BackYardigans." *Vox Daily* (blog), Voices. com, September 6, 2006. http://blogs.voices.com/voxdaily/2006/11/alicia_keys_guest_ stars_on_the_backyardigans.html.

The album's singles were also a commercial success. "You Don't Know My Name," "If I Ain't Got You," "Diary," and "Karma" reached the top twenty of the Billboard Hot 100.

The reviews of *The Diary of Alicia Keys* were mainly positive. It received a rating of 71 out of 100 on Metacritic. The positive reviews focused on how Keys mixed different types of sounds. "There are so many facets to this album. In addition to the trademark earthy organic sound, we are also treated to an eclectic mix of genres," wrote Denise Boyd, a reviewer for the British Broadcasting Corporation (BBC). "From cosmic jazz to sensual salsa she has it covered. I for one am very glad that Alicia Keys has revealed the secrets of her diary."[44] Not all listeners, however, found everything in her album positive. Josh Tyrangiel wrote in *Time* magazine,

Keys accepts the Best R&B Video award for "If I Ain't Got You" at the 2004 MTV Video Music Awards.

On The Diary of Alicia Keys she has made half a great record. The first six songs are models of how to make nostalgic music that is not anti-present. "You Don't Know My Name" is six minutes of sprawling midtempo lightness that revives that '70s staple, the spoken interlude, without a moment's embarrassment or doubt; "Karma" uses fraught bursts of strings over a stuttering beat to create great pop tension; while "If I Was Your Woman" sounds like the product of a one-night stand between Gladys Knight (who made a hit of "If I Were Your Woman") and the Notorious B.I.G. The second half of Diary sags.[45]

The Diary of Alicia Keys and its songs received several awards, including the MTV Award for Best R&B Video for "If I Ain't Got You" and Grammy Awards for Best R&B Album, Best Female R&B Vocal Performance for "If I Ain't Got You," Best R&B Song for "You Don't Know My Name," and Best R&B Performance by a Duo or Group with Vocals for "My Boo," which she sang with Usher.

Verizon Ladies First Tour

Keys did not go on tour for her second album like she did for her first. Instead she participated in the 2004 Verizon Ladies First Tour, which featured Keys, Missy Elliott, and Beyoncé. During the tour, they performed at twenty different venues in March and April.

The tour earned over $20 million, one of the biggest tours in 2004 and received positive reviews. During the concerts, Keys performed after Elliot. According to reviewer Neil Drumming,

Alicia Keys met Missy's energy head-on with ramped-up renditions of her typically mellow material. But Keys was at her best—albeit most self-indulgent—solo and spotlit behind a baby grand, belting out melodrama. Her old-school references charmed, and her clap-along "How Come You Don't Call Me" obliterated the CD version. Mounting the piano, tickling keys with one hand, she struck a quirky balance between class and kitsch.[46]

Keys performs in Florida in March 2004 on the Verizon Ladies First Tour, which she co-headlined with Missy Elliot and Beyoncé Knowles.

The performers said that they got along well, and there were no jealousies or issues with one another during the tour. All three had worked or dealt with one another at different points earlier in their careers. "What a lot of people don't realize is that I've known Beyoncé since we were both at Columbia Records and we used to do showcases together," Keys said. "And I was just with Missy at the Brit Awards where we performed (Prince's song "Kiss") with [singer] Gwen Stefani."[47]

Alicia Keys: Unplugged

Keys's next musical endeavor after the Verizon Ladies First Tour was to make another album. She selected her most popular songs from her first two albums and some new songs to create *Alicia Keys: Unplugged*. Keys recorded the album live in July 2005 at the Brooklyn Academy of Music in Brooklyn, New York. The performance was also filmed as an episode of the popular MTV television show *Unplugged*, which showcases top performers

Keys performs at the Brooklyn Academy of Music in July 2005 to record her Unplugged *album as part of an episode of the popular MTV series.*

playing their music live. During her performance, Keys was joined onstage by Common, Mos Def, Damian Marley, and Adam Levine. "Throughout this consistent set, marked by warmth, sincerity and a powerful lack of inhibition, Keys convinces that if she's not the new [singing and songwriting legend] Aretha Franklin, she's a force of equal might and measure," wrote Amazon.com reviewer Tammy La Gorce. "All the favorites are here, the danceable 'Karma' carries into the funky 'Heartburn' and the give-it-up glory of 'Unbreakable.' 'Fallin', 'If I Ain't Got You,' and 'You Don't Know My Name' come later, but interspersed are enough pleasant surprises to make even fanatical Keys followers forget the signature songs."[48]

In September 2005, the show aired on MTV, and on October 11, 2005, J Records released the album. It debuted on the Billboard 200 chart at number one. In its first week the album sold 196,000 copies in the United States. It was the highest selling debut for an MTV *Unplugged* album since 1994. Since its release, the album has sold over 1 million copies in the United States and over 2.5 million copies worldwide. "Unbreakable," a single on the album, reached the top ten for the Billboard 100. *Alicia Keys: Unplugged* garnered four Grammy Award nominations.

A New Goal

To keep herself in shape, Alicia Keys works out and exercises on a regular basis. One day she decided to take her regular routine a step further. In 2006 she completed her first marathon in Greece. "I just kind of woke up and thought, 'I want to run a marathon.' So we started preparing for it and I did! It was the weirdest sensation. It was pretty long—it took me five hours!"

Quoted in "Alicia Keys—Smokin' Aces Motivated Keys to Run Marathon." Contactmusic. com, January 23, 2007. www.contactmusic.com/news/smokin-aces-motivated-keys-to-run-marathon_1019787.

A State-of-the-Art Studio

With all of her musical success, Keys decided the next step was to set up her own, state-of-the-art music studio. In 2005 she worked with Kerry "Krucial" Brothers and a team to take an existing New York recording studio and make it state of the art with the latest high-end recording equipment. While the recording studio was up-to-date and modern, it was located in an old house in a calm neighborhood lined with trees. Keys chose it for the atmosphere because she wanted a relaxing place to work.

To make sure she got the type of studio she envisioned, Keys and Krucial worked with engineer Ann Mincieli, who gathered a team that included David Malekpour of Professional Audio Design and John Storyk, Beth Walters, Dirk Noy, and Chris Bowman of Walters-Storyk Design Group, an architectural and acoustical design firm. The team created Keys and Krucial's studio, called The Oven.

The Oven has a 230-square-foot (21-square-meter) control room and includes several different types of amps and other equipment. All of the cables are out of sight, using an under-the-floor routing scheme. In the room next to the control room is a 535-square-foot (50-square-meter) space with a stone wall and a staged floor plan set up for Keys's vocal and piano works. Keys wanted this studio so she could have full control over creating her sound. "I've always written, I've always played the piano, and when I heard these songs in my head, I would know what I wanted the feel and the sound to be," said Keys "Krucial was one of the first people to encourage me to take things into my own hands. That's why producing is so important to me. I'm able to hear my thoughts and voices, and I can present it as only I know it should exist."[49]

Writing Poetry

Keys loves to write, which is one of the reasons she is passionate about music. She writes her own songs. In 2004 she decided to do more than just write lyrics. She wrote poetry and released it as a book, *Tears for Water: Songbook of Poems and Lyrics*. The title of the book comes from the line "I don't mind drinking my tears for

Keys attends a book signing for **Tears for Water: Songbook of Poems and Lyrics,** *which she published in* **2004.** *The book made the* **New York Times** *bestseller list the following year.*

water" from her poem "Love and Chains." Keys said, "And when I read [that line], it resonated in me because I said, 'Wow, I realized at that moment that all of the songs I write, all of the poetry that I write, every way that I express myself comes from some form of my tears, my pain, my happiness, my joy, my frustration, my confusion.' And I drink them for water to be nourished and to survive, in a way."[50]

Reviews of her book were mixed. Reviewer Troy Patterson of *Entertainment Weekly* magazine was not impressed. He wrote, "The patient reader winces mildly at flat laments about alienation ('Sometimes I feel/like I don't belong anywhere') and emotional reticence ('I'm a prisoner/Of words unsaid/Just lonely feelings/Locked away in my head')—poems sometimes followed by Keys' own explanations of their 'meanings.' Serviceable metric patterns are as scarce as vivid images, or signs of shame."[51] Despite some negative reviews, Keys's book was a commercial success. The book made the *New York Times* bestseller list in 2005.

Keys's interest in writing led to the *New York Daily News* asking her to be a travel correspondent. During her 2004 summer world tour, she wrote about the places she visited for the newspaper. Her tour included a performance at the Great Wall of China with other performers, such as pop singer Cyndi Lauper. Keys wrote about how these places inspired her. By visiting other countries she was able to see how different cultures lived, and she wrote about it in her posts. "Away from America, things are so historic," said Keys. "Touring gives me the opportunity to see the people, the faces, the eyes. The song of it, the sound of it, is all very inspiring to me."[52]

Personal Beliefs

Keys's personal beliefs inspire both her writing and music. When talk-show host Oprah Winfrey interviewed her in 2004, she opened up about her thoughts on important topics, such as religion. "I feel the presence of a higher power," Keys said. "I believe that what you give is what you get. It's universal law. I believe in the power of prayer and of words. I've learned that when you predict that negative things will happen, they do. And I pray about 75 times a day."[53] She said that her ideas about religion and life end up in her music.

Keys's ideas about the world also appear in her music. Keys told Winfrey about how she wants her music to open people's eyes to what is happening in the world. "There's no formula to my music, it's just rooted in my heart and soul. Whether I talk about visiting the pyramids in Egypt, to witnessing the AIDS epidemic in Africa or matters of the heart everyone will be able to experience where I've been and where I am going in my life."[54]

Keys believes that people need to give back to the world. As busy as her writing and music career keep her, she still finds time to help others. In addition to continuing her work with Keep a Child Alive, Keys became involved in other charities. In 2005 she teamed up with the nonprofit organization Frum tha Ground Up to assist teens in learning the importance of self-worth and direction. She visited inner-city schools and talked with students about her own journey. In 2006 she became the organization's

Keys speaks in a classroom in Chicago, Illinois, in 2005 as part of her work with Frum Tha Ground Up, one of several charities she supports.

spokesperson. She also became involved with Teens in Motion, an organization in the South Bronx, New York, that provides a safe environment for teens to dance, sing, act, and participate in self-esteem workshops.

By the end of 2005 Keys was busy with her charity work, writing, and music. She continued to make goals in all her areas of interest and started to think about new projects. Keys had more to say and more to do.

Chapter 4

New Endeavors

After three successful albums, tours, and a book, Keys wanted to try new projects. She decided to expand her career as a performer by doing something she had loved as a child—acting. Growing up, Keys took acting lessons and appeared in cameos on some television shows. Keys decided to try acting again, as an adult.

Movie Debut

When director Joe Carnahan heard that Keys was interested in acting, he decided he wanted her in his movie. "She was playing at the Paramount in Oakland [California], and I drove up there to see her," Carnahan said. "I watched her show, which was fantastic, and I went backstage. . . . I sat down and talked to her, and I said, 'They are going to come to you with some . . . romantic comedy. Don't do it. Read this instead!' Well, she had read it at that point, and said, 'Wow, it's really intense,' and I said, 'Yeah, so, do you want to shake things up?'"[55] Keys made her movie debut in Carnahan's *Smokin' Aces*, which premiered in January 2007.

In *Smokin' Aces*, a crime thriller, Keys plays a hit woman. She agreed to the role because most people would expect a musician, when first entering the movie business, to choose a movie that focuses on music. Keys wanted to try something completely different. In the movie Keys performs with veteran actors Ryan Reynolds, Ben Affleck, Andy Garcia, and Ray Liotta. Despite her lack of acting experience, Keys was confident on the movie set.

Keys poses with a gun as part of her role as a hit woman in the 2007 movie Smokin' Aces. ***Keys enjoyed learning how to shoot a gun for the part.***

One of the things Keys enjoyed about the movie was that she got to learn new things, such as how to shoot a gun. "I can absolutely handle a gun in real life," Keys said. "My trainer told me that I might be the best one on the set in regards to the handling of gunfire. Not only did I train with weapons, but I trained physically for the part as well."[56]

Unfortunately, the movie was not a great success. The reviews for *Smokin' Aces* were mainly unfavorable. On Rotten Tomato, a website that tracks reviews of movies, only 28 percent of critics gave the movie favorable reviews.

Keys's next movie role was in the comedy *The Nanny Diaries*, which premiered in August 2007. Like *Smokin' Aces*, *The Nanny Diaries* received mostly critical reviews. Even though the reviews were not good, Keys was glad for the opportunity to act in another movie. She liked having the chance to play another character. "That's part of the appeal of acting, being able to just totally dive into another portion of your personality," Keys said. "Because we're *all* made up of so many different personalities. That is an incredible feeling."[57]

Needing a Break

While Keys was working on her movies, she learned that her paternal grandmother was diagnosed with cancer, an illness that eventually claimed her life. The diagnosis made Keys pause and reflect. "It made me finally stop," she said. "Nothing else was more important—no work, no costumes, no anything. I was forced to slow down, look at my life, and decide who I wanted to be. It all got very low at first because I was very depressed and I didn't understand why."[58] Keys

Keys hugs her grandmother, Vergil DiSalvatore, in 2003. Her grandmother's death in 2006 prompted Keys to take a break from her career.

decided she needed a break, and in the fall of 2006, after her grand-mother died, she took a trip to Egypt by herself. She got a guide to lead her to different sights and historic places for over a month. She swam in the Red Sea, visited the pyramids, and took a cruise on the Nile River. For the most part people did not recognize her, and she was able to stay anonymous as she traveled. This gave her time to think about what she wanted to do next.

The trip refreshed Keys and gave her a new perspective on life. She returned to New York ready to make a new album reflecting her personal growth. "It gave me a new sense of power, free-dom, creativity, and limitlessness," she said. "When I came back [to New York], I was so much more clear. I didn't want to feel so closed and internal," said Keys. "I wanted to enjoy life and explore the possibilities of life. And that's when I started doing music for [my next] album."[59]

Gaining Confidence

Although Keys was ready to make a new album, she wanted to do it at her own pace. She no longer wanted to work so hard that she was exhausted. She had gained the confidence to tell people if she disagreed with a proposed schedule. Although she was still dedicated to her work, Keys felt confident that she did not have to work all the time in order to succeed.

Her new confidence also extended to her appearance. She got rid of her trademark braids and adopted a hairstyle of curls and waves and began to wear more elegant clothes. "It's not like I was consciously like, I want to make a change," she said. "It just natu-rally started happening with my freedom of expression, [gaining] more confidence, and letting go."[60]

Keys put this confidence into her new album, *As I Am*. The title of the album reflects who Keys had become at that point. Her increased confidence in herself led to her being more upfront with others. "I'm done with being a person that doesn't understand themselves because it's being detrimental to my health and my spirit and my mind," said Keys. "Everybody's in trouble now because I will tell it like it is."[61]

Keys adopted a more glamorous, sophisticated look in 2007, reflecting a newfound confidence that also affected her approach to making As I Am.

Making *As I Am*

Keys made her new album at her studio, The Oven. She worked with many performers and musicians who had strong musical backgrounds to create the album. Her main collaborator was her coproducer, Kerry "Krucial" Brothers, whom she had worked with since her first album. She also worked with Linda Perry from the band the 4 Non Blondes on the song "Superwoman," which includes lyrics about women coming together. She also worked with John Mayer on "Lesson Learned." Jamaican bassist

John Mayer, right, collaborated with Keys on the song "Lesson Learned," one of the tracks on As I Am.

and producer Robbie Shakespeare, from the duo Sly and Robbie, also performs with Keys on the album.

Photos of musicians, including Nina Simone, Janis Joplin, and Bob Marley, line the walls of Keys's studio for inspiration, and the influence of those in the photos is reflected in *As I Am*, as Keys mixes up her classic soul sound with pop and rock. Some songs are rooted in gospel music and updated with deeper bass and programmed drumbeats. Keys said that she feels a connection to the music of the 1960s and 1970s, and this connection is evident in the songs on the album.

The first single on *As I Am*, "No One," is about her break from being a star, when she went to Egypt to regroup. According to Tammy La Gorce, a reviewer for Amazon.com, "No One" is a "firestorm of a song clearly born of a sore heart and steeped in serious soul-searching. . . . [It] was about her decision to retreat from the obligations of stardom when she found out a loved one was in need of her care. . . . There's only one way R&B artists grow to become legends, and it's by drenching the words they sing with feeling."[62]

Reaction to *As I Am*

J Records heavily promoted *As I Am* prior to its release. The marketing campaign included advertisements on MTV's television channel and website. *As I Am* also streamed on MTV's website on November 6, 2007, a week before its official release. The week of the album's release Keys was MTV's Artist of the Week.

J Records released *As I Am* on November 13, 2007. The promotions paid off because *As I Am* was a commercial success. It debuted at number one on the Billboard 200 chart and sold 742,000 copies in its first week. Four singles from the album topped the charts and "No One" became the most-listened to song of 2007 in the United States. "No One" also became Keys's third number-one hit single. By 2011 it had sold over 11 million copies worldwide.

Keys accepts one of the two Grammys she won in 2008 for the song "No One."

Gangsta Rap Controversy

At times Alicia Keys's opinions have caused controversy. In 2008 *Blender* magazine quoted her as saying that gangsta rap was a "ploy [by the U.S. government] to convince black people to kill each other." Many people criticized her for being anti-American and for making baseless claims against the U.S. government. Because of the controversy, Keys eventually had to clarify what she said. "My comments about 'gangsta rap' were in no way trying to suggest that the government is responsible for creating this genre of rap music," Keys said in a statement issued by J Records. "The point that I was trying to make was that the term was oversloganized by some of the media causing reactions that were not always positive. Many of the 'gangsta rap' lyrics articulate the problems of the artists' experiences and I think all of us, including our leaders, could be doing more to address these problems."

Quoted in "Keys's Side of the Story." *Chicago Tribune*, April 16, 2008. http://articles. chicagotribune.com/2008-04-16/news/0804160672_1_rap-blender-alicia-keys.

Critically the album did not perform as well as Keys's past albums. Metacritic gave the album a score of 66 out of 100. Edna Gundersen, a reviewer with *USA Today*, gave the album three out of four stars, noting that Keys did not experiment with any new sounds. "She may be playing it safe with this radio-friendly batch of midtempo R&B, but Keys also plays it straight, never striking a false emotional note as she serves up gorgeous ballads and steamy soul,"[63] wrote Gundersen. J. Freedom du Lac of the *Washington Post* newspaper thought that the album was disjointed and the lyrics generic. "*As I Am*, which is uneven, unfocused and never gets around to answering the critical question of exactly what—or, rather, who—Keys is, other than a 27-year-old artist still in search of an identity,"[64] he wrote.

Negative criticism did not keep the album from getting awards. Keys received two Grammy Awards for the song "No One":

Best Female R&B Vocal Performance and Best R&B Song. She also received four NAACP Image Awards: Outstanding Album, Outstanding Female Artist, Outstanding Song for "Like You'll Never See Me Again," and Outstanding Music Video for "Like You'll Never See Me Again".

As I Am Worldwide Tour

In 2008 Keys embarked on a worldwide concert tour for *As I Am*. The tour began in England on February 28 and ended in Australia on December 20, with a month off in November. During the U.S. leg of her tour, Keys had to cancel some concerts due to swollen vocal chords.

Jordin Sparks, one of the winners on *American Idol*, a singing competition television show, was the opening act for Keys's U.S. shows. The concert mixed songs from *As I Am* with older favorites. Keys performed some songs simply by singing and playing the piano while other songs were big production numbers. The production numbers included an eight-piece band, several dancers, and Keys, who danced while singing.

The reviews of her *As I Am* tour were mixed. Some felt that Keys was not herself the entire time onstage. Joan Anderman, a reviewer with the *Boston Globe* newspaper, thought that Keys shined when she just sang and played the piano but that the other parts of the show were overproduced and did not seem authentic. "Keys isn't a dancer or a ringleader," Anderman wrote after seeing the concert in Boston. "She's a writer and singer of songs. And while her time behind the piano may not have fulfilled the modern cultural ideal of what an R&B superstar does on a stage, those quieter, less visceral moments made a strong case for sticking with your strengths."[65]

Branching Out

Throughout her year of touring, Keys found time to embark on other projects. One was to work with guitarist and singer Jack White of the band the White Stripes, known for hard-rock music.

Keys and Jack White, right, recorded the song "Another Way to Die" for the 2008 James Bond film Quantum of Solace.

Keys and White worked together to record "Another Way to Die," the theme song for the James Bond film, *Quantum of Solace* (2008). It was the first Bond movie theme song performed as a duet.

White recorded "Another Way to Die" in his Nashville, Tennessee, studio, while Keys added piano and vocals. The song is a mixture of guitar alternative rock and hip-hop rhythms played against orchestral brass and strings. In the video for the song Keys plays on a white upright piano, while White alternates between guitar and drum kit. "Alicia put some electric energy into her breath that cemented itself into the magnetic tape. Very inspiring to watch," said White. "You're definitely taking on a responsibility. There's a tradition of powerful music in all these [James Bond] films. But that's why I'm involved creatively with music, for challenges like this."[66]

White and Keys were not the first choice to record the theme song. Originally, singer Amy Winehouse was asked to create and perform the song, but she had personal problems and could not get a song recorded in time. Although they were not first choice, White and Keys created a song that was a commercial success. It reached the Billboard 100, and it was the thirteenth official Bond theme to appear on the Hot 100.

The Secret Life of Bees

Although *Smokin' Aces* and *The Nanny Diaries* gave Keys a taste for acting, it was awhile before she had time to work on another movie. In 2008 she found time. Keys accepted a part in *The Secret Life of Bees*, a film based on the book of the same name by Sue Monk Kidd. Having read and appreciated the book, Keys was excited to play a part in the movie. Set in the South during the 1960s, the movie centers on teenager Lily Owens and her nanny, who leave their hometown to uncover the mysteries of Lily's late mother. They end up staying with the Boatwright sisters.

Keys plays June, one of the Boatwright sisters, and she had to learn to play the cello for the part. Once she learned that, she enjoyed playing June, a strong female character. Keys also thought the energy on the set was positive. "Everybody was very

Keys performs a scene from the 2008 film The Secret Life of Bees.

On *Oprah*

Alicia Keys has a small role in the 2008 movie *The Secret Life of Bees*. In October 2008, the same month in which the movie was released, Keys and some members of the cast appeared on the television show, *The Oprah Winfrey Show*. On the show Keys talked about how she always wanted to push herself to improve in all she does in life. "I never want to ever find myself too comfortable anywhere, because I don't think you can grow if you're too comfortable," Keys explained to Oprah. "Even with my music, I like to do things that I'm not quite comfortable with, because it pushes me to do better."

Quoted in *"The Secret Life of Bees'* Cast." Oprah.com, October 2, 2008. http://www.oprah.com/oprahshow/The-Secret-Life-of-Bees-Cast_2.

excited about the piece and really into it for all the right reasons," Keys said. "So it was a great energy and everyone kind of stepped up to the plate with a boldness and a confidence and a certain gentleness too that just made it really human."[67]

Released in October 2008, the film received more positive reviews than Keys's previous movies and garnered the NAACP Image Award for Outstanding Motion Picture. Keys earned a nomination for Outstanding Supporting Actress in a Motion Picture for her performance, but did not win.

Commercial Projects

In addition to all her other endeavors, Keys also became a product promoter. In March 2008 she starred in a small series of commercials, sponsored by Dove, a brand of products including soap, deodorant, shampoo, conditioner, and lotion, made by the Unilever company. The series marked the launch of Dove go fresh, a fragrance-driven product collection.

The series consisted of three-minute commercials that broadcast nationwide over a five-week period starting in March 2008 during the television show *The Hills*, which aired on MTV. The commercials follow three twenty-something female friends as they deal with their careers, relationships, beauty, families, friends, and self-doubts. The women realize that feeling confident and happy with their relationships and who they are is what makes them feel beautiful. Keys said, "I hope the series inspires other 20-somethings to get a fresh take on the pressures in their lives and start enjoying the ride."[68]

A few months after the Dove go fresh commercials, Keys agreed to become the spokesperson for Glacéau, vitaminwater. Keys agreed to represent the product, because she actually drank it and felt it benefited her health. She was reportedly paid over $25 million.

Continuing with Charity

Keys continued to raise money and awareness for Keep a Child Alive. She produced the documentary, *Alicia in Africa: Journey to the Motherland*, which debuted on the cable channel, Showtime. The goal of the film is to educate people about the problems of children affected by AIDS in Africa and give them ideas about what they can do to help. In 2008 Keys and Keep a Child Alive released the film as a free download on the Internet so everyone can view it. Keys also shows a clip from the film during her concerts to encourage fans to make a donation.

Another documentary, *Keep a Child Alive with Alicia Keys*, follows Keys as she visits Uganda, Kenya, and South Africa. With Keys are Americans Talaina Brown, Kristen Dyer, Rachel Hathaway, Aaron McCoy, and Sonya Soni, who won the chance to travel with her. The film documents the people they meet and the major problems they are dealing with because of AIDS.

With her work and her charity, Keys was managing a busy life. Her multitasking skills would soon be challenged as major changes took place in her personal life.

Chapter 5

Marriage, Motherhood, and More

For years, Keys focused on her work. This changed in 2008 when she worked in her studio with Kasseem Dean, who goes by the name Swizz Beatz.

Keys first met Dean as a teenager, when they were both starting their careers in the music industry. By 2008 Dean had become a successful music producer, and he and Keys fell in love while working together. "Our relationship definitely grew from a friendship," Keys said. "It's really beautiful to be understood without a lot of excess talking. With Kasseem, I can be my true self, and he can be his true self and we shine equally. When we are in the same room, nobody falls in the shadow."[69]

Keys was able to relax with Dean, and she got better at putting her work aside and enjoying other parts of life. As time passed, their relationship grew more serious.

A Complicated Situation

Falling in love with Dean was, unfortunately, complicated. He was married, although he had separated from his wife in April 2008. Then in May 2008 a woman who was not his wife gave birth to his child. Dean's wife, Mashonda Tifrere, claims Keys broke up her

Keys and Beatz, left, appear at an event in 2010. Although they had met years earlier, they became a couple after they began working together in 2008.

DJ Keys

On a night out, in November 2011, Alicia Keys became a DJ during a party at Yotel in New York City. Her husband, Swizz Beatz, was spinning the records when Keys took over. The crowd cheered when they saw her. She played Black Moon, Gangstarr, Pete Rock, and CL Smooth and, according to attendees at the party, seemed at ease playing the "ones and twos," otherwise known as the DJ turntable.

marriage and destroyed her family. Keys says that she and Dean did not begin dating until after he separated from Tifrere.

For the most part Keys kept silent. She was happy to have found a relationship with Dean and tried to focus on that. "I was aware of all the false things being said about me," she said. "But I was sure if I engaged [said something], it would become back-and forth like some sort of sick entertainment, which goes against everything I believe in and only would have made things worse. Of course people will believe what they want to believe. But I know the truth will shine through."[70]

More Work to Be Done

Her relationship with Dean did not keep Keys from her music. In 2009 she began to work on the album *The Element of Freedom* at The Oven. On this album she sang about the emotions she felt in 2006 when her grandmother died. When interviewed, she said that the album allowed her to show both her strong and vulnerable sides. "I found more freedom. Before, I thought I could only show the strong side of me. Now there's a mixture of strong and delicate," Keys explained. "A new sound, a new emotion."[71]

Keys said different types of music inspired her during the recording of her fourth album. During this time, she listened to artists such as Genesis, Tears for Fears, Fleetwood Mac, and The Police. The result was a music style that includes more 1980s and 1990s pop and techno sounds. Her acoustic piano playing is still heard on much of the album, but some songs also include electronic drums and synthesizer sounds.

During the time she worked on *The Element of Freedom*, Keys also collaborated with other artists on different projects. She and singer Jay-Z worked together to create the song, "Empire State of Mind," which reached number one on the Billboard singles chart. Keys also recorded her own version of the song, "Empire State of Mind (Part II) Broken Down," for *The Element of Freedom*.

Keys also collaborated with Spanish recording artist Alejandro Sanz on the song "Looking for Paradise." The single is included on Sanz's eighth album. Keys, along with Dean, also wrote and produced "Million Dollar Baby," a song with a disco feel, for singer Whitney Houston.

Another Successful Album

J Records released *The Element of Freedom* in December 2009. Commercially, the album was a success even though it was Keys's first album that did not debut at number one on the Billboard 200. Instead it debuted at number two and sold 417,000 copies in its first week. Eventually it sold over 1 million copies in the United States, and the Recording Industry Association of America certified it platinum.

The first single Keys released from the album was "Doesn't Mean Anything." It reached number sixty on the Billboard Hot 100 chart. Her second single released from the album, "Try Sleeping with a Broken Heart," received positive reviews for its use of beats and 1980s sounds. It reached number twenty-seven on the Billboard Hot 100. Keys's most successful song from the album was "Un-Thinkable (I'm Ready)," which reached number twenty-one on the Billboard Hot 100.

The Element of Freedom received many favorable reviews, and Metacritic rated it 67 out of 100. Several reviewers found the album more natural and well-rounded than her previous albums.

Greg Kot, a reviewer for the *Chicago Tribune*, did not agree. He wrote, "She aims to go deeper on 'Freedom,' adopting a more measured, mid-tempo approach and a more introspective tone. Keys has said the album is about overcoming depression, presumably after a bad break-up. But the lyrics are so trite it's difficult to buy into the album as a personal statement."[72]

The main criticism of her album was that her songwriting was safe and unchanging. Despite the criticism, most critics agreed that her voice helped carry the album. Leah Greenblatt wrote in *Entertainment Weekly*, "What Keys' often-banal lyrics lack, her quicksilver voice carries."[73]

Keys attends an event in January 2010 to promote the release of The Element of Freedom.

The Element of Freedom did not receive any Grammy Award nominations nor did any of its singles. Keys did receive two Grammy Awards, Best Rap/Sung Collaboration and Best Rap Song, for "Empire State of Mind" in 2010.

Freedom Tour

Keys followed the release of The Element of Freedom with a world tour. The tour began in Canada in February 2010 and continued until July 2010. Europe, North America, and South Africa were included on the tour. Most of the performances were about an hour and a half long and included twenty-two songs. Throughout

Jay-Z and Keys stand for applause after performing "Empire State of Mind" together at her concert at Madison Square Garden in New York in March 2010.

the tour Keys added some special touches. At her concert at Madison Square Garden in New York City, Beyoncé performed "Put It in a Love Song." Later in the show Swizz Beatz and Jay-Z performed with Keys on "Empire State of Mind." At her concert in Arnhem, Netherlands, she asked the audience to say "Happy Birthday Mama Keys" in honor of her mother's birthday.

The reviews of this tour were similar to Keys's past tours. Several reviewers thought Keys was at her best when singing her ballads and playing the piano as opposed to when she sang and danced in theatrical numbers. "If that piano had kept talking, it probably would've advised Keys to stay right there. Whenever Keys took a seat, her concert took off," wrote Kot. "One of the best-selling artists of the last decade, Keys is a classically trained pianist with neo-soul vocal chops who is best served by keeping things small and relatively intimate. But in her concerts, she also tries to compete with spectacle-heavy peers such as Beyoncé, Pink and Christina Aguilera."[74]

American Idol

Even while touring, Keys found time for another project. In April 2010 she appeared as a mentor on *American Idol*. Keys helped contestants during their rehearsals by giving them advice and tips.

During the week she mentored, Keys also performed on the show's "Idol Gives Back" special, a fund-raiser for Children's Health Fund, Feeding America, Malaria No More, Save the Children, and other U.S. charities. Keys sang her singles "Unthinkable" and "Empire State of Mind" live onstage. The annual event raised nearly $45 million.

Becoming a Wife and Mother

In the spring of 2010, Dean bought a seven-carat engagement ring and proposed to Keys. They were married on July 31, 2010, on the French island of Corsica. The wedding was a small affair, with sixty close friends and family as guests. Keys wore an ivory silk, one-shoulder gown by designer Vera Wang and carried a

A pregnant Keys arrives with Beatz at the Keep a Child Alive Black Ball in September 2010. She gave birth to son Egypt the next month.

bouquet of purple calla lilies. She walked down the aisle with both her mother and father.

Following Keys's marriage to Dean, another major personal event occurred in her life. She and Dean became parents to Egypt Daoud Dean on October 14, 2010, in New York. They named their son Egypt because of her 2006 experience in Egypt.

Keys discussed being a mother on her blog just two weeks after giving birth. Usually reserved about her personal life, Keys opened up about what it felt like to be a new mother. "I can spend HOURS looking at one little EAR! Have u ever noticed how complex just an ear is? A tiny maze of art. It may sound silly but it's so true. Or a heartbeat?" she wrote. "Everyday we wake up and in some way, take for granted the fact that this beautiful pulsating organ in our body is the reason, and yet now that's all I can think of."[75]

Keys admits that Egypt has helped her become a more open person. She believes that motherhood has given her a more relaxed attitude about life. "I was very closed for a long time," she explained. "But I feel so open now. To feel open like this means you've found the center in yourself. You're not hiding, you're not worried about anything."[76]

And More Work

Balancing work and motherhood soon became a part of Keys's life. Shortly after giving birth, Keys got back to work. She decided to focus more on her acting and directing projects. In early 2011 she began to work on the documentary, *Five*, an anthology of five short films that depict the impact of breast cancer on the lives of five women. Keys was asked to direct one of five short films for the project. Each film depicts the life of a different breast cancer sufferer. Actresses Jennifer Aniston and Demi Moore also directed films for the project.

Keys decided to do the project because she feels that breast cancer is an important subject. She was able to choose which short film and character to direct, and she selected Lili because Keys felt a connection to her. Keys's film follows Lili, a career-minded woman played by actress Rosario Dawson, who is diagnosed with

Keys poses with fellow directors Jennifer Aniston, left, and Demi Moore, right, at the premier of Lifetime's Five in September 2011.

The Power of Women

Alicia Keys has a website that offers news about her career and her charities. It also has a blog, where Keys expresses her thoughts and feelings about various issues. Since becoming a mother, she has thought a lot about the effect that women have in the world. In February 2011 she let her readers know the power she believes that women have. "Because without the wonders of a woman, nothing would grow as tall, nothing would be built as big, nothing would be so fragrant, or shine as bright," Keys wrote. "So the more I think about it, the more I'm certain that a woman's love is the most powerful force in the world."

Alicia Keys. "AK Blogs: The Most Powerful Force in the World." *Alicia's Blog,* February 23, 2011. www.aliciakeys.com/us/news/ak-blogs-most-powerful-force-world.

breast cancer. Her relationships with her mother and sister are a main part of the film. "After I read the scripts, I felt like this was something important, and I wanted to be a part of it," Keys said. "I chose Lili because she's close to my age and I understood the family dynamic. I had an immediate idea of what I could bring to it."[77] *Five* premiered on the Lifetime cable television network on September 26, 2011.

Music not Forgotten

In 2011 Keys began working on her next album. She discovered that the process of making an album is different now that she is a mother. She used to write songs late into the night at her studio. Now Keys writes more songs at home with Egypt in a chair by her feet.

In September 2011, she gave a preview of one of her new songs while playing at the iHeartRadio Music Festival in Las Vegas. "I've

Keys performs at the iHeartRadio music festival in Las Vegas, Nevada, in September 2011. During the show, she premiered a new song titled "A Place of My Own."

been in the studio working on some new music, and I thought tonight would be the perfect night to play something new for you," Keys told the audience. "Is it OK for me to play something brand-new? Yes, let's do it."[78] She then sang "A Place of My Own" while playing the piano. The song is about building up the courage to overcome struggles and find happiness.

The album will be her first that is not released by J Records. This is because in October 2010 RCA disbanded J Records along with two other labels. Keys and all other artists associated with the three labels will release any future material on another RCA Records brand.

In June 2011, *Songs in A Minor* was rereleased in a deluxe edition and in a collector's edition to commemorate the album's tenth anniversary. Keys promoted the release by going on a short, four-city tour, titled Piano & I: A One Night Only Event with Alicia Keys. The tour featured only Keys, singing and playing her piano.

In late 2011 Keys combined music and the theater by becoming producer and composer for *Stick Fly*, a Broadway play. The play is about an affluent African American family that comes together to spend a weekend at their mansion on Martha's Vineyard, an island that is a part of Massachusetts. Keys expressed excitement at composing the music for the show. "As someone who walked up and down this boulevard as a young girl, I cannot describe the thrill of having the opportunity of composing songs for a Broadway show," said Keys. "It's honestly been a dream come true. I love the humor and humanity of *Stick Fly*, and I'm so excited to be a part of the emotional journey this show will take audiences on."[79]

More Charity Work

Keys always finds time for her charity, Keep a Child Alive. She wants to set an example for Egypt and teach him to be a person who gives to the world. "I think as a compassionate person, which I really want to teach him to be, you naturally want to lend and be a part of change," Keys explained. "I know that naturally he'll find the thing that he's passionate about and wants to change."[80]

As of 2012, Keep a Child Alive continues to grow. Since its founding in 2003, the charity has provided HIV/AIDS drugs to more than 250,000 adults and children in Africa, and it has raised more than $28 million. In May 2011 Keys asked readers of her blog to check out the Keep a Child Alive website. Every day in the month of May, Keep a Child Alive shared a story about a child, mother, or family affected by HIV/AIDS that was served by the agency's work.

In November 2011 Keys hosted the annual Black Ball event to raise funds for Keep a Child Alive. Many of Keys's friends played at the event including Usher, will.i.am, Jay Sean, Clark, and Norah Jones. Additionally, Keys managed to get several celebrities to donate experiences with them, such as a dinner party for 10 with Naomi Watts, to sell at the live auction. The event raised over three million dollars for Keys's charity.

Keys speaks at the 2011 Black Ball supporting Keep a Child Alive, which has provided antiretroviral drugs to more than 250,000 people with HIV/AIDS since it was founded in 2003.

Although Keep a Child Alive is the charity closest to her heart, Keys also finds time for other charities, such as the Stephen Lewis Foundation, which supports AIDS/HIV prevention in Africa. In 2011 she performed at a fund-raising event for the foundation, the Hope Rising! Concert in Toronto, Canada, along with artists such as K'Naan, Angelique Kidjo, Rufus Wainwright, and Holly Cole. Keys performed three songs, "New York," "Fallin'," and "No One." Keys also gives back locally. In November 2011 she donated musical instruments to her old school, the Professional Performing Arts School in Manhattan.

Charity, music, performing arts, and family are the main components of Keys's life. Achieving success in all of these areas has taken focus, talent, and hard work. As long as she continues on this path, the world will see much more from Alicia Keys.

Introduction: A Veteran at Age Thirty

1. Alicia Keys. "News." *Alicia's Blog*, April 12, 2011. www.aliciakeys. com/us/alicia-keys-blog.
2. Quoted in Jay Smith. "Alicia Keys's Special Night." Pollstar, May 3, 2011. www.pollstar.com/blogs/news/archive/2011/ 05/03/766318.aspx.

Chapter 1: What Music Means

3. Quoted in Ria Higgins. "Relative Values: Alicia Keys, R&B Singer, and Her Mother, Terri Augello, Actress," *Sunday Times* (London), June 6, 2004. www.thesundaytimes.co.uk/sto/ public/sitesearch.do?querystring=alicia+keys+ria+higgins& sectionId=2&p=sto&bl=on&pf=all.
4. Quoted in Akin Ojumu. "Soul Sister." *Guardian*, November 16, 2003. www.guardian.co.uk/music/2003/nov/16/aliciakeys.
5. Quoted in "Oprah Talks to Alicia Keys." Oprah.com, September 2004. www.oprah.com/omagazine/Oprahs- Interview-with-Alicia-Keys.
6. Quoted in Ojumu, "Soul Sister."
7. Quoted in Asian News International. "Music and Dance Kept Alicia Keys Out of Trouble During Childhood." Thaindian News, July 15, 2008. www.thaindian.com/newsportal/sports/ music-and-dance-kept-alicia-keys-out-of-trouble-during- childhood_10071626.html.
8. Quoted in Janet Mock and Julia Wang, eds. "Celebrity Central: Alicia Keys." *People*, 2011. www.people.com/people/ alicia_keys.
9. Quoted in Higgins. "Relative Values."
10. Quoted in "Oprah Talks to Alicia Keys."
11. Quoted in "Oprah Talks to Alicia Keys."
12. Quoted in "Alicia Keys." ASCAP. www.ascap.com/playback/2005/ summer/features/keys.html.

13. Quoted in "Penguin Prison Interview: I Get Sad When Dogs Are Crying." *RobotPigeon* (blog), June 8, 2010. www. robotpigeon.com/2010/06/penguin-prison-interview-i-get-sad-when.html.
14. Quoted in Jon Pareles. "To Be Alicia Keys: Young, Gifted and in Control." *New York Times*, January 27, 2002. www.nytimes. com/2002/01/27/arts/music-to-be-alicia-keys-young-gifted-and-in-control.html?src=pm.
15. Quoted in "Oprah Talks to Alicia Keys."
16. Quoted in Higgins. "Relative Values."
17. Quoted in Lynn Norment. "Alicia Keys: Sounds Off on Men, Love & Fame." *Ebony*, January 2004, p.134.
18. Quoted in "Oprah Talks to Alicia Keys."
19. Quoted in "Oprah Talks to Alicia Keys."
20. Quoted in "Oprah Talks to Alicia Keys."
21. Quoted in "Oprah Talks to Alicia Keys."

Chapter 2: A Successful Beginning

22. Quoted in Stephanie Merritt. "Soul Sister Number One." *Guardian*, March 21, 2004. www.guardian.co.uk/music/2004/mar/21/popandrock.aliciakeys.
23. Quoted in "Newcomer Alicia Keys Chooses 'Songs in A Minor.'" Billboard.com. www.billboard.com/news/newcomer-alicia-keys-chooses-songs-in-a-895768.story#.
24. Quoted in Norment. "Alicia Keys."
25. Quoted in "Newcomer Alicia Keys Chooses 'Songs in A Minor.'"
26. Quoted in "Newcomer Alica Keys Chooses 'Songs in A Minor.'"
27. Steve Jones. "Travis, Made Manifest R&B's Alicia Keys Hits All the Right Ones." *USA Today*, June 12, 2001.
28. Quoted in Pareles. "To Be Alicia Keys."
29. Quoted in "'I Love Chopin. He's My Dawg.'" *Guardian*, November 1, 2001. http://www.guardian.co.uk/lifeandstyle/2001/nov/02/shopping.artsfeatures9.
30. Quoted in Pareles. "To Be Alicia Keys."
31. Quoted in Merritt. "Soul Sister Number One."
32. Quoted in Pareles. "To Be Alicia Keys."

33. Quoted in Norment. "Alicia Keys."
34. Quoted in Norment. "Alicia Keys."
35. Quoted in Pareles. "To Be Alicia Keys."
36. Quoted in TOURÃ. "Alicia Keys The Next Queen of Soul." *Rolling Stone*, November 10, 2001. www.rollingstone.com/music/news/alicia-keys-the-next-queen-of-soul-20011108.
37. "Biography." AliciaKeys.com. www.aliciakeys.com/us/alicia-keys-biography.

Chapter 3: Onward and Upward

38. Quoted in Corey Moss. "Road to the Grammys: The Making of *The Diary of Alicia Keys*." MTV, February 8, 2005. www.mtv.com/news/articles/1496693/road-grammys-alicia-keys.jhtml.
39. Quoted in Moss. "Road to the Grammys."
40. Quoted in Moss. "Road to the Grammys."
41. Quoted in Moss. "Road to the Grammys."
42. Quoted in Moss. "Road to the Grammys."
43. "Biography."
44. Quoted in Denise Boyd. "Alicia Keys: The Diary of Alicia Keys Review." BBC, August 19, 2003. www.bbc.co.uk/music/reviews/bg63.
45. Josh Tyrangiel. "Alica Keys: The Princess of Queens." *Time*, December 8, 2003. www.time.com/time/magazine/article/0,9171,1006405-1,00.html.
46. Neil Drumming. "Tour Report: Ladies First." EW.com, April 2, 2004. www.ew.com/ew/article/0,,604994,00.html.
47. Quoted in Steve Jones. "For Ladies of Hip-hop, R&B, a Musical 'First.'" *USA Today*, March 9, 2004. www.usatoday.com/life/music/news/2004-03-09-ladies-first-inside_x.htm.
48. Tammy La Gorce. "Editorial Reviews: Amazon.com." CD review. Amazon.com. www.amazon.com/Mtv-Unplugged-Alicia-Keys/dp/B000B5IPLK.
49. Quoted in David Weiss. "The Oven Studios." MIX, October 1, 2005. http://mixonline.com/mag/audio_oven_studios.
50. Quoted in Brian Dakss. "The Poetry of Alicia Keys." CBSNews, February 11, 2009. www.cbsnews.com/stories/2004/11/11/earlyshow/leisure/celebspot/main655152.shtml.

51. Troy Patterson. "Tears for Water." EW.com, November 5, 2004. www.ew.com/ew/article/0,,735551,00.html.

52. Quoted in Greg Baker. "Alicia Keys Plays at Great Wall of China." *USA Today*, September 24, 2004. www.usatoday.com/life/people/2004-09-24-keys_x.htm.

53. Quoted in "Oprah Talks to Alicia Keys."

54. Quoted in Carla Hay. "Alicia Keys Epitomizes Freedom of Expression." *Examiner*, January 28, 2010. www.examiner.com/celebrity-q-a-in-national/alicia-keys-epitomizes-freedom-of-expression.

Chapter 4: New Endeavors

55. Quoted in Larry Carroll. "'Aces' Director Says Alicia Keys, Common Give Him the Upper Hand." MTV, November 3, 2006. www.mtv.com/news/articles/1544780/alicia-keys-common-give-aces-upper-hand.jhtml.

56. Quoted in Larry Carroll and Jeff Cornell. "Alicia Keys Kills—Literally—in Film Debut, 'Smokin' Aces.'" MTV, January 2, 2007. www.mtv.com/news/articles/1548928/alicia-keys-kills-film-debut-smokin-aces.jhtml.

57. Quoted in "For Alicia Keys, Hollywood Stardom Beckons from the Pages Of 'The Nanny Diaries.'" MTV, June 29, 2006. www.mtv.com/news/articles/1535392/alicia-keys-primed-her-screen-debut-with-scarlett.jhtml.

58. Quoted in Margeaux Watson. "The Agony & Ecstasy of Alicia Keys." EW.com, November 28, 2007. www.ew.com/ew/article/0,,20160311,00.html.

59. Quoted in Watson. "The Agony & Ecstasy of Alicia Keys."

60. Quoted in Watson. "The Agony & Ecstasy of Alicia Keys."

61. Quoted in Jon Pareles. "A Neo-Soul Star as She Is: Nurturing Her Inner Rebel," *New York Times*, September 9, 2007. http://www.nytimes.com/2007/09/09/arts/music/09pare.html?pagewanted=1.

62. Quoted in Tammy La Gorce. "Editorial Reviews: Amazon.com." CD review. Amazon.com. www.amazon.com/As-I-Am-Alicia-Keys/dp/B000VEYJP2.

63. Edna Gundersen. "'As I Am' Is Alicia Keys at Her Most Skillful." *USA Today*, November 13, 2007. www.usatoday.com/life/music/reviews/2007-11-12-alicia-keys_N.htm.

64. J. Freedom du Lac. "Alicia Keys, Still Warming Up." November 13, 2007. *Washington Post*. www.washingtonpost.com/wp-dyn/content/article/2007/11/12/AR2007111201967.html.

65. Joan Anderman. "Keys Shines in Soulful Tunes, but Overproduction Dims Luster." Boston.com, June 12, 2008. http://articles.boston.com/2008-06-12/ae/29279839_1_jermaine-paul-alicia-keys-soulful-singer.

66. Quoted in Neil McCormick. "Quantum of Solace: Jack White Helps Alicia Keys Put a Bomb under James Bond." *Telegraph* (London), September 24, 2008. www.telegraph.co.uk/culture/music/3561149/Quantum-of-Solace-Jack-White-helps-Alicia-Keys-put-a-bomb-under-James-Bond.html.

67. Quoted in Marie Morreale. "*The Secret Life of Bees*: Alicia Keys." Scholastic, October 24, 2008. www.scholastic.com/browse/article.jsp?id=3750639.

68. Quoted in "Alicia Keys and Dove Give Women a Fresh Take on Life in Their Twenties." Press release. PR Newswire, March 24, 2008. www2.prnewswire.com/mnr/dove/32409.

Chapter 5: Marriage, Motherhood, and More

69. Quoted in Jeannine Amber. "Alicia in Love." *Essence*, June 2011, p. 127.

70. Quoted in Amber. "Alicia in Love," p. 127.

71. Quoted in The Improper. "Alicia Keys Tackles Depression with Fourth Album." The Improper Music, December 2, 2009. www.theimproper.com/music/142/alicia-keys-tackles-depression-with-fourth-album.

72. Greg Kot. "Album Review: Alicia Keys, 'The Element of Freedom.'" *Chicago Tribune*, December 13, 2009. http://leisureblogs.chicagotribune.com/turn_it_up/2009/12/album-review-alicia-keys-the-element-of-freedom.html.

73. Leah Greenblatt. "The Element of Freedom." EW.com, December 9, 2009. http://www.ew.com/ew/article/0,,20326058,00.html.
74. Kot. "Album Review."
75. Alicia Keys. "I Feel a Song Coming On." *Alicia's Blog*, October 26, 2010. www.aliciakeys.com/us/alicia-keys-blog/i-feel-song-coming.
76. Quoted in Amber. "Alicia in Love," p. 128.
77. Quoted in "Glamour Interview: Jennifer Aniston, Demi Moore and Alicia Keys Talk!" *Glamour*. www.glamour.com/health-fitness/2011/09/glamour-interview-jennifer-aniston-demi-moore-and-alicia-keys-talk?currentPage=5.
78. Quoted in James Dinh. "Alicia Keys Debuts New Song At iHeartRadio Festival." MTV, September 26, 2011. www.mtv.com/news/articles/1671482/alicia-keys-place-of-my-own-i-heart-radio-festival.jhtml.
79. "Alicia Composes Music for Stick Fly on Broadway." AliciaKeys.com, October 18, 2011. www.aliciakeys.com/us/news.
80. Quoted in Derrick Bryson Taylor. "Alicia Keys Wants to Raise a Charitable Son." *Essence*, November 6, 2011. www.essence.com/2011/11/06/alicia-keys-wants-to-raise-a-charitable-son.

1981

Keys is born in New York, New York.

1985

Appears on *The Cosby Show*.

1993

Attends the Professional Performing Arts School.

1994

Jeff Robinson hears Keys sing and becomes her manager.

1997

Graduates as valedictorian from the Professional Performing Arts School.

1999

Leaves Columbia Records and signs with J Records.

2001

Songs in A Minor debuts at number one on the Billboard 200 chart.

2002

Wins five Grammy Awards for *Songs in A Minor*.

2003

J Records releases *The Diary of Alicia Keys*.

2005

Performs on *MTV Unplugged* and J Records releases *Unplugged*.

2007

J Records releases *As I Am*. Keys makes her film debut in *Smokin' Aces*.

2008

The Secret Life of Bees, a movie in which Keys has a supporting role, is released.

2009

J Records releases *The Element of Freedom*.

2010

Marries Swizz Beatz and gives birth to son Egypt.

2011

A collector's edition of *Songs in A Minor* are released to commemorate the album's tenth anniversary.

Books

Terrell Brown. *Alicia Keys*. Broomall, PA: Mason Crest, 2007. This book is about Keys's life and career.

Geoffrey Horn. *Alicia Keys*. New York: Gareth Stevens, 2005. This biography details Keys's early life and her career in the years immediately following the release of *Songs in A Minor*.

Alicia Keys. *Tears for Water: A Songbook of Poems and Lyrics*. New York: Berkley Trade, 2005. This book is a mixture of lyrics from Keys's albums and poetry.

Periodicals

Jeannine Amber. "Alicia in Love." *Essence*. June 2011. The article is an interview with Keys about marriage and motherhood.

David Browne. "Alicia Keys Looks Back on a Decade of Monster R&B Hits." *Rolling Stone*, March 4, 2010. This article gives Keys input on her music.

Marti Parham. "Celebrating Her 'Womanhood' Singer Alicia Keys Discusses Music, Marriage & Making a Difference." *Jet*, December 3, 2007. This is an interview with Keys about her thoughts on different subjects.

Websites

AliciaKeys.com (www.aliciakeys.com). This is Alicia Keys's official website. It provides the latest news and information about her projects and includes a blog written by Keys.

MTV (www.mtv.com/music/artist/keys_alicia/artist.jhtml) This website offers information about the music industry and Alicia Keys.

Keep A Child Alive (http://keepachildalive.org/). The official website for the charity that Keys is so passionate about. It has background on the organization as well as information on how to get involved and how to donate.

Leanne Currie-McGhee has enjoyed writing nonfiction for over a decade. She lives in Norfolk, Virginia, with her beautiful daughters, Grace and Hope, and supportive husband, Keith.